COLORING BOOKS
FOR BOYS
ANIMAL DESIGNS

▲ ART THERAPY COLORING

Preview of Coloring Pages

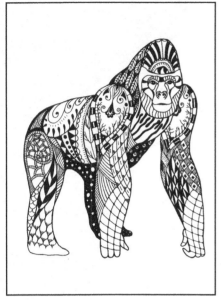

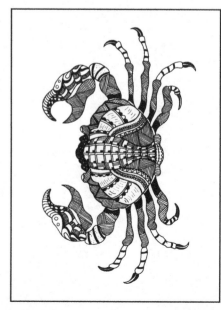

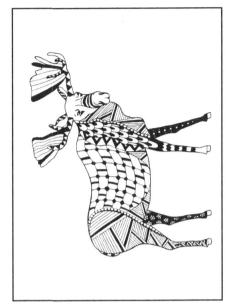

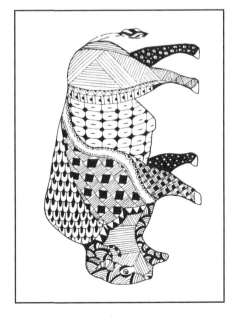

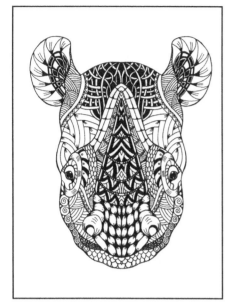

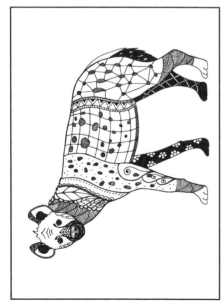

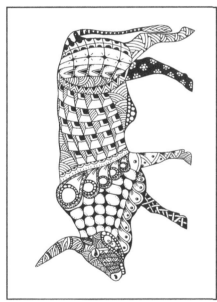

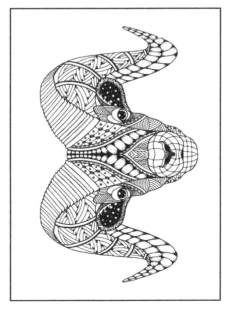

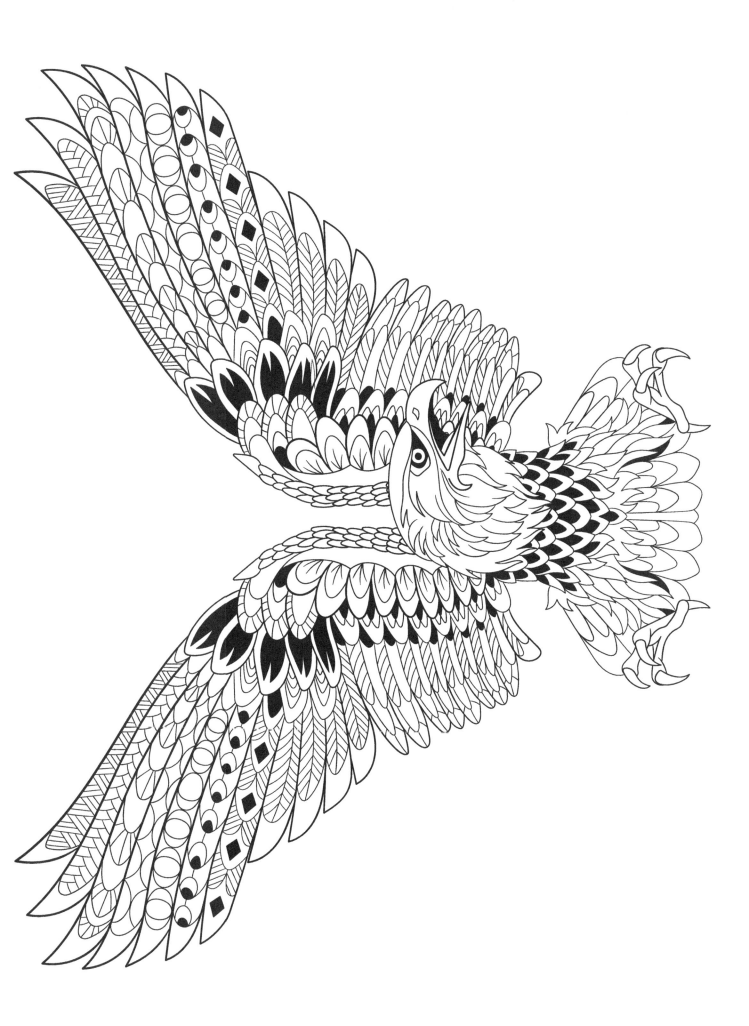

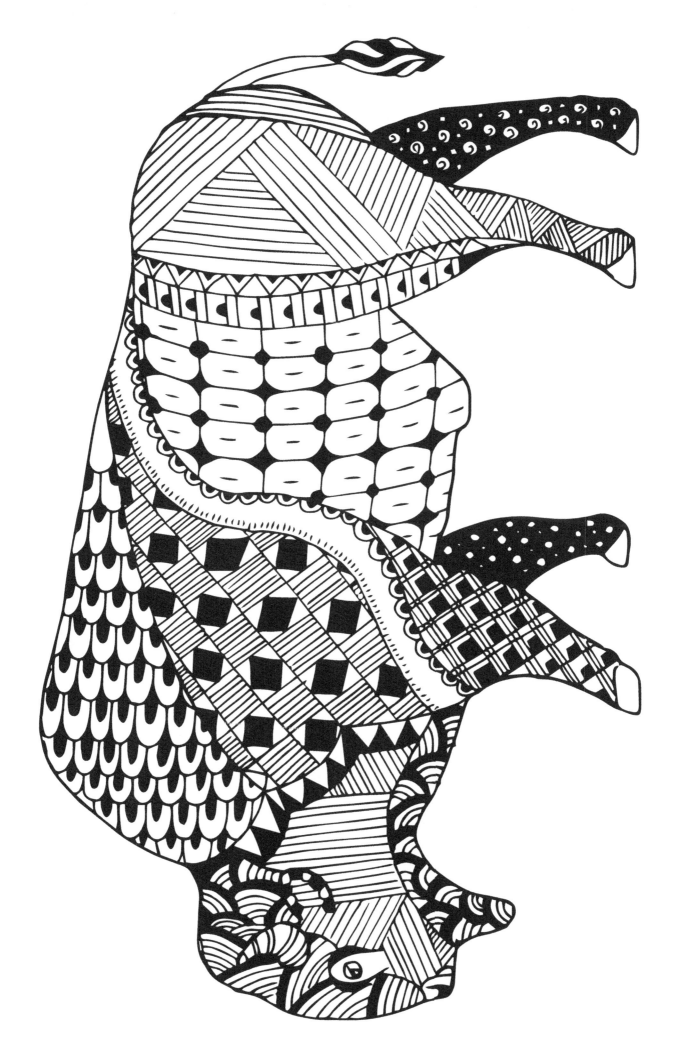

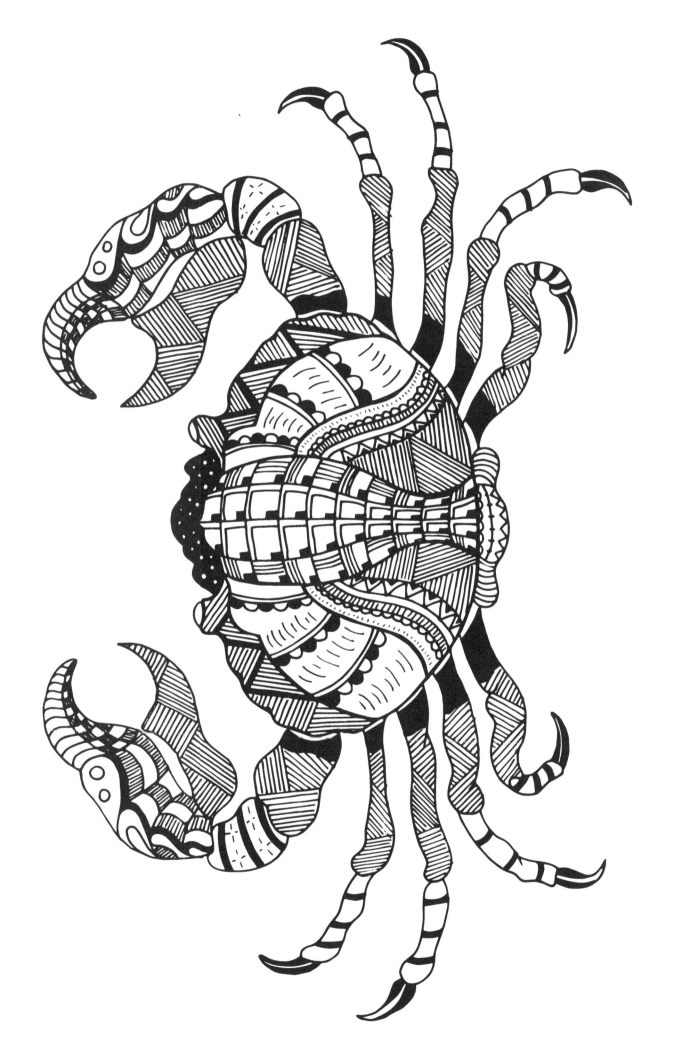

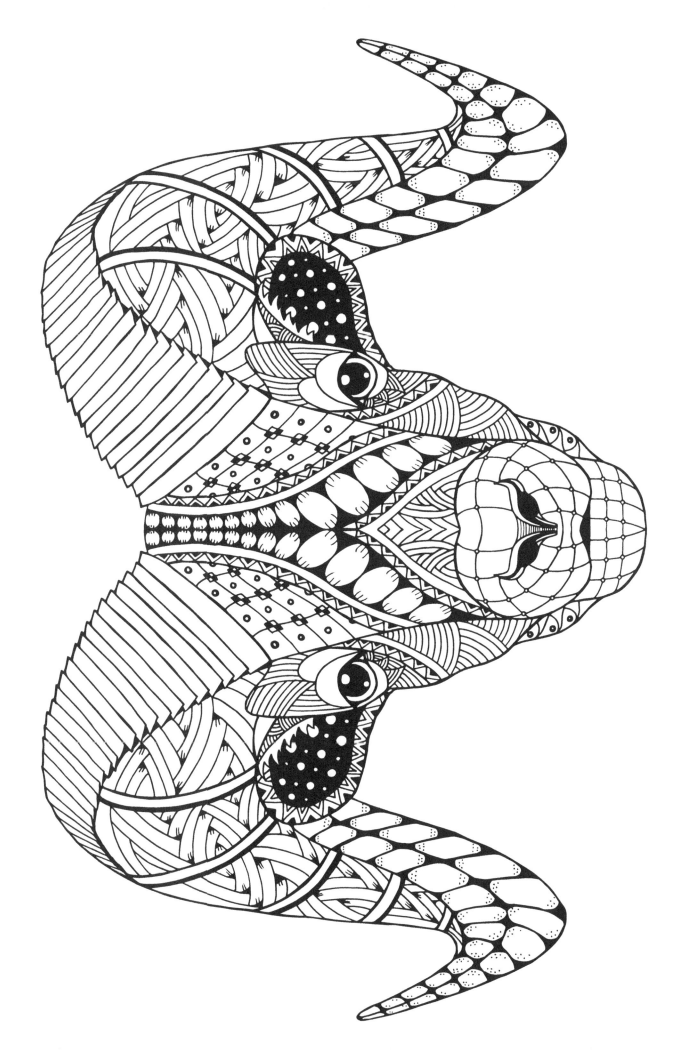

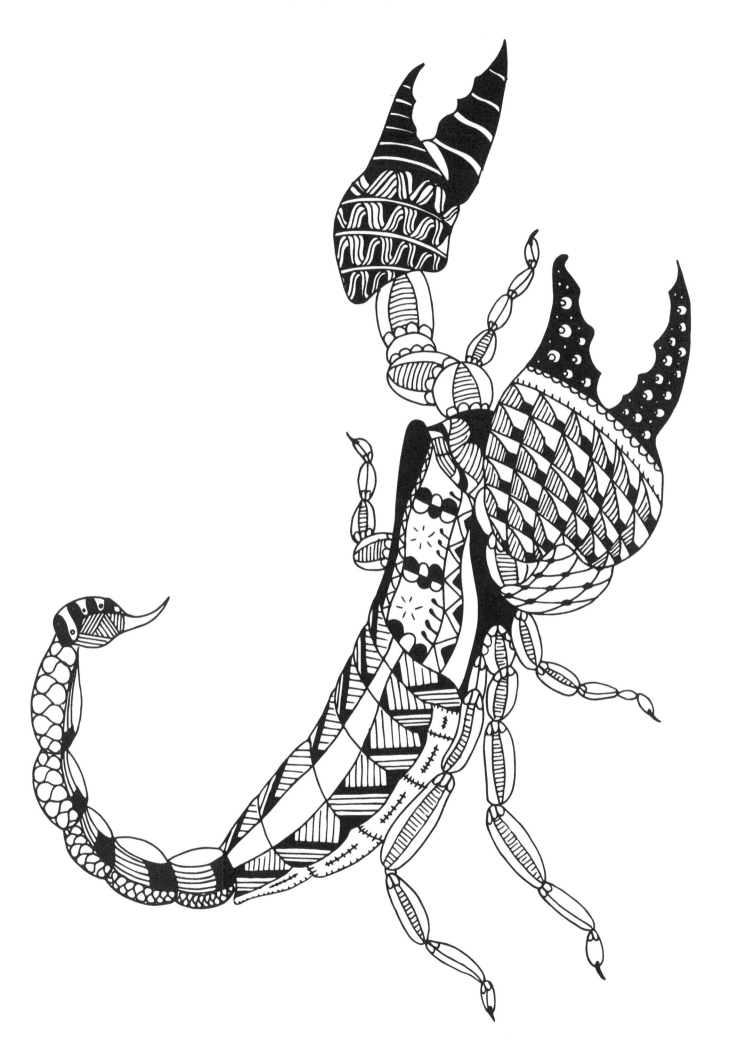

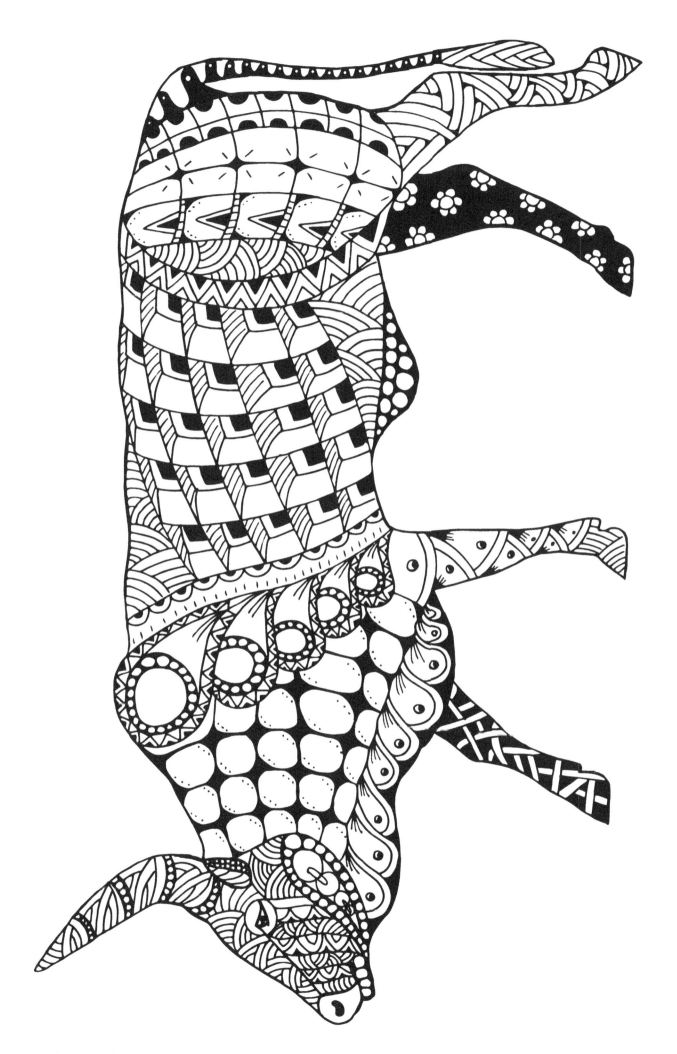

Test Your Colors

Best Selling Art Therapy Coloring Books

Coloring Books For Adults:

- Zombie Coloring Book: Black Background
- Butterfly Coloring Book For Adults: Black Background
- Tattoo Coloring Book: Black Background
- Coloring Books for Adults Relaxation: Native American Inspired Designs
- Fishing Coloring Book for Adults: Black Background

Coloring Books For Men:

- Coloring Book for Men: Anti-Stress Designs Vol 1
- Coloring Book For Men: Fishing Designs
- Coloring Book For Men: Tattoo Designs
- Coloring Books for Men: Hunting
- Coloring Book For Men: Biker Designs

Coloring Books For Seniors:

- Coloring Book For Seniors: Nature Designs Vol 1
- Coloring Book For Seniors: Anti-Stress Designs Vol 1
- Coloring Books for Seniors: Relaxing Designs
- Coloring Book For Seniors: Floral Designs Vol 1
- Coloring Book For Seniors: Ocean Designs Vol 1

Coloring Books For Teens and Tweens:

- Coloring Books For Teens: Ocean Designs
- Coloring Books for Teen Girls Vol 1
- Teen Inspirational Coloring Books
- Coloring Book for Teens: Anti-Stress Designs Vol 1
- Tween Coloring Books For Girls: Cute Animals

Coloring Books For Kids:

- Horse Coloring Book For Girls
- Coloring Books For Boys: Sharks
- Coloring Books for Boys: Animal Designs
- Unicorn Coloring Book for Girls
- Detailed Coloring Books For Kids

Art Therapy Coloring Books

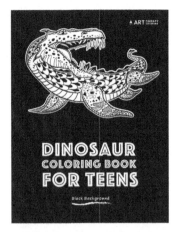

DINOSAUR
COLORING BOOK
FOR TEENS
Black Background

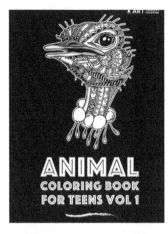

ANIMAL
COLORING BOOK
FOR TEENS VOL 1

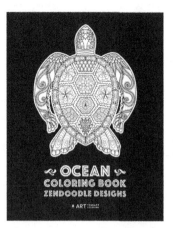

OCEAN
COLORING BOOK
ZENDOODLE DESIGNS

MERMAID
COLORING BOOK
FOR TEENS
Black Background

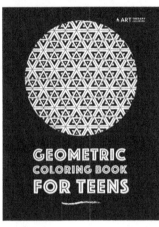

GEOMETRIC
COLORING BOOK
FOR TEENS

SKULL
COLORING BOOK
FOR TEENS
Black Background

ANIMAL
COLORING BOOK
FOR TEENS VOL 2

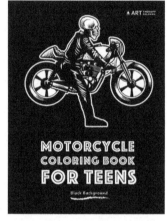

MOTORCYCLE
COLORING BOOK
FOR TEENS
Black Background

Tween Coloring Books For Girls
Black Background Vol 1

Tween Coloring Book
Black Background Vol 1

Coloring Book For Tweens
Black Background Hearts

THE ISLAND LIFE

Coloring Book For Tweens
Ocean Patterns Vol 2

Tween Coloring Book
Skull Designs

Tween Coloring Book
Mermaid & Ocean Designs

Tween Coloring Book
Ocean, Pirate, Skulls

Coloring Book For Tweens
Ocean Patterns Vol 1

Art Therapy Coloring Books

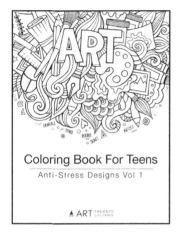

Coloring Book For Teens
Anti-Stress Designs Vol 1

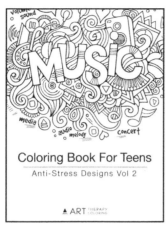

Coloring Book For Teens
Anti-Stress Designs Vol 2

Coloring Book For Teens
Anti-Stress Designs Vol 3

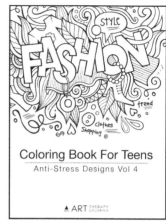

Coloring Book For Teens
Anti-Stress Designs Vol 4

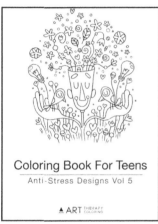

Coloring Book For Teens
Anti-Stress Designs Vol 5

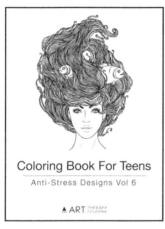

Coloring Book For Teens
Anti-Stress Designs Vol 6

Coloring Book For Teens
Anti-Stress Designs Vol 7

Coloring Book For Teens
Anti-Stress Designs Vol 8

Teen Coloring Book
Stress Relieving Designs

Tween Coloring Books For Girls
Stress Relief Vol 1

Tween Coloring Books For Girls
Stress Relief Vol 2

Tween Coloring Book
I Love You!!!

Tween Coloring Book
Wolves, Lions, Tigers

Tween Coloring Book
Dragon Designs

Art Therapy Coloring Books

COLORING BOOKS
FOR BOYS
WILD ANIMALS
ART THERAPY COLORING

COLORING BOOKS
FOR BOYS
DRAGONS
ART THERAPY COLORING

COLORING BOOKS
FOR BOYS
ANIMAL DESIGNS
ART THERAPY COLORING

COLORING BOOKS
FOR BOYS
OCEAN DESIGNS
Black Background

COLORING BOOKS
FOR BOYS
SHARKS
ART THERAPY COLORING

DINOSAUR
COLORING BOOKS
FOR BOYS
Detailed Designs

COLORING BOOKS
FOR BOYS
NATIVE AMERICAN INSPIRED
ART THERAPY COLORING

COLORING
BOOKS FOR BOYS
ANIMALS
ART THERAPY COLORING

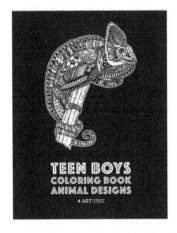

TEEN BOYS
COLORING BOOK
ANIMAL DESIGNS
ART THERAPY COLORING

TEEN COLORING BOOKS
FOR BOYS
DETAILED DESIGNS
ART THERAPY COLORING

TEEN COLORING BOOKS
FOR BOYS
DETAILED DESIGNS
Black Background

COLORING BOOKS
FOR TEEN BOYS
DETAILED DESIGNS
ART THERAPY COLORING

COLORING BOOKS
FOR TEEN BOYS
DETAILED DESIGNS
Black Background

ADULT
COLORING BOOKS
FOR KIDS
Geometric Designs

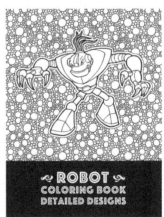

ROBOT
COLORING BOOK
DETAILED DESIGNS

DETAILED
COLORING BOOKS
FOR KIDS
Geometric Designs

Art Therapy Coloring Books

Tween Coloring Book

Wolves, Lions, Tigers

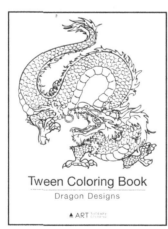

Tween Coloring Book

Dragon Designs

Tween Coloring Book

Ocean, Pirate, Skulls

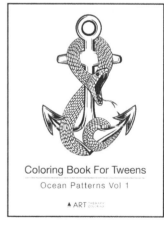

Coloring Book For Tweens

Ocean Patterns Vol 1

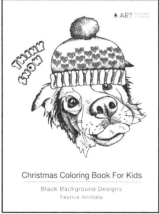

Christmas Coloring Book For Kids

Black Background Designs
Festive Animals

Christmas Coloring Book For Kids

Detailed Designs Vol 1

Christmas Coloring Book For Kids

Detailed Designs Vol 2

Christmas Coloring Book For Kids

Detailed Festive Designs

Coloring Books For Boys
Animal Designs

Published by:
Art Therapy Coloring
www.arttherapycoloring.com

Shutterstock Images

ISBN: 978-1-64126-027-5

Made in the USA
Monee, IL
31 March 2023

31015219R00050